j636.13　Gammie, Janet L.
GAM
　　　　　Palomino horses.

$17.07

DATE			

BAKER & TAYLOR

HORSES

PALOMINO HORSES

JANET L. GAMMIE

ABDO & Daughters

Published by Abdo & Daughters, 4940 Viking Drive, Suite 622, Edina, Minnesota 55435.

Library bound edition distributed by Rockbottom Books, Pentagon Tower, P.O. Box 36036, Minneapolis, Minnesota 55435.

Printed in the United States.

Cover Photo credit: Peter Arnold, Inc.
Interior Photo credits: Peter Arnold, Inc.

Edited by Bob Italia

Library of Congress Cataloging-in-Publication Data

Gammie, Janet L.
    Palomino Horses/ Janet L. Gammie.
        p.   cm. — (Horses)
Includes bibliographical references (p.23) and index.
    ISBN 1-56239-442-8
    1. Palomino horse—Juvenile literature.   [1. Palomino horse. 2. Horses.] I. Title. II.
Series: Gammie, Janet L. Horses.
SF293.P3G36 1995
636.1'3—dc20   95-5448
                                                                       CIP
                                                                       AC

ABOUT THE AUTHOR

Janet Gammie has worked with thoroughbred race horses for over 10 years. She trained and galloped thoroughbred race horses while working on the racetracks and farms in Louisiana and Arkansas. She is a graduate of Louisiana Tech University's Animal Science program with an equine specialty.

Contents

WHERE PALOMINOS CAME FROM

Horses are mammals just like humans. Mammals are warm-blooded animals with a backbone. Their body heat comes from inside their body.

The horse's earliest **ancestor** was *Eohippus* (e-oh-HIP-us). It lived about 50 million years ago. The palomino was **bred** from Spanish horses in the United States and Mexico.

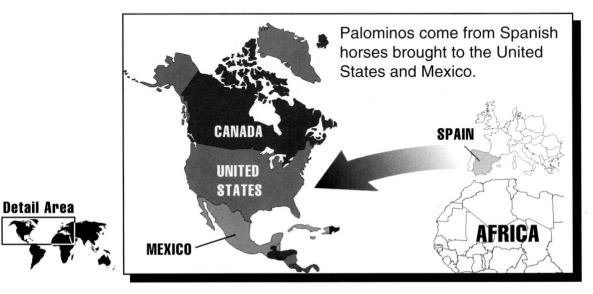

Palominos come from Spanish horses brought to the United States and Mexico.

Detail Area

CANADA

UNITED STATES

MEXICO

SPAIN

AFRICA

The palomino horse.

The palomino's golden color may have been around for as long as horses have been **domesticated**. In the 1940s the palomino became a horse **breed**. The most famous palomino is Roy Rogers' horse, "Trigger."

WHAT PALOMINOS LOOK LIKE

Palominos are not a true horse **breed.** They are a color breed. A true breed is a horse group from one family, like the Arabian. A color breed can be made up of many different horse families. But it must be a certain color.

Palominos are from stock or light horse breeds. Stock horses are **quarter horses** and **thoroughbreds**. A light horse breed is any true horse breed other than quarter horse and thoroughbred.

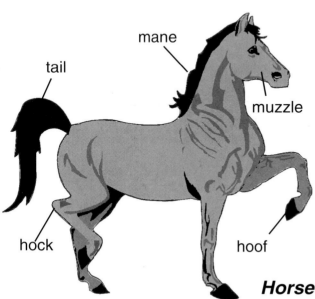

Horses share the same features.

Palominos are of light horse breeding.

Palominos are 14 to 17 hands high (hh). Each hand equals 4 inches (10 centimeters). Their weight depends on their breeding.

WHAT MAKES PALOMINOS SPECIAL

A palomino's quality and type depends on **breeding**. Almost half the palominos are **quarter horses**. Quarter horses have wide heads with a small **muzzle**. Their ears are short and set far apart. They have large dark eyes. Their bodies are heavily muscled.

The other half of the palomino family is from different breeding. This includes the saddle horse, **thoroughbred**, Morgan, Tennessee Walker, and the **saddlebred**.

Making the palomino color is hard. Breeding two palominos makes palomino **foals** only half of the time. The other foals are born chestnut and cremello (off-white) color.

The palomino's body is very muscular.

COLOR

The palomino is the true "golden" horse. It is a golden color with a flaxen mane and tail. Flaxen is white with some darker hairs mixed in.

Palominos are of two types. One type has dark or black skin, the other has light skin. All palominos have black, brown or glass eyes. Glass eyes are blue or hazel in color. There are no stripes or spots on the body.

Palomino **markings** are a solid white hair patch on the head and legs. There are five basic head markings: star, stripe, snip, blaze and bald face. Leg markings include ankle, sock and stocking. Palominos can have any mix of head and leg markings.

STAR   STRIPE   SNIP   BLAZE   BALD FACE

The palomino is known as the "golden" horse.

CARE

Except for horses that are working, showing, or racing, most horses are happier living on **pasture**. Horses kept on pasture or in stalls are vaccinated and **dewormed** often. A vaccination is a shot that protects the horse from disease. Deworming rids the horse of parasites inside the body. Parasites are bugs that live off another animal, causing sickness.

After a horse is two years old the teeth are floated. Floating is filing the teeth so they are even. This allows for proper chewing of food. A horse's **hooves** are trimmed often just like people trim their fingernails. Hoof trimming begins when the horse is about five months old.

Good grooming habits protect the horse from parasites that live on the skin and hair. Grooming is brushing and cleaning the horse's body.

Palominos living in stalls must be vaccinated.

FEEDING

Horse feed includes hay, grain and water. Hays are alfalfa and grass. Each type of hay offers different **nutrition**. Alfalfa is higher in **protein** than the grasses. Alfalfa and grass hays can be mixed together. Grains include oats, corn, barley and wheat. Different hay and grain amounts are fed depending on how active the horse is and how much it has grown.

Pregnant mares, **weanlings** and working horses need extra feed. Weanlings are **foals** 4 to 6 months old that are not **nursing**. Fresh, clean water should always be given.

Palominos feed on hay and grass. They also need plenty of water.

THINGS PALOMINOS NEED

The saddle protects a horse's back and makes riding smoother. There are two basic saddle types: the **Western saddle** and the **English saddle**.

The **bridle** and **bit** give the rider control. There are five basic bridle and bit types: the snaffle, double bridle, Pelham, gag, and bitless.

The snaffle bit has a mouth piece that can be jointed in the middle or whole. It is the easiest of all bits on the horse's mouth. The double bridle has two bits and two sets of **reins**. The two bits and reins are used separately. The Pelham also has two bits but they act as one.

The gag bit is a snaffle bit that has one bit but two sets of reins. It is the bit to wear. The bitless bridle does not have a bit. The bitless bridle puts pressure on the horse's nose. Bit control puts pressure on the horse's mouth.

The saddle protects a palomino's back and makes riding smoother.

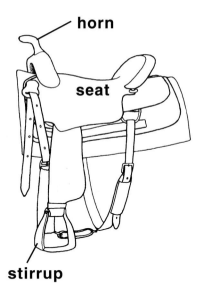

horn

seat

stirrup

THE WESTERN SADDLE

17

HOW PALOMINOS GROW

Foals live inside the **mare's** body for about 11 months. The foal can stand 15 minutes after birth. Within two hours the foal will **nurse**.

Foals develop fast. They can live without the mare's milk after 3 to 4 months. At that time they are taken away from the mare. The foal is then called a **weanling**. Weanlings are put together in one pasture. They spend the next few months playing, eating and sleeping.

Horses can sleep standing up. The horse locks its leg joints so that it does not fall down. By sleeping standing up they are always ready to run away from danger. Horses also sleep lying down. But they are never in this position for long.

Within two hours of being born the foal will nurse from the mare.

TRAINING

Horses learn more easily when young. **Training** should begin shortly after birth. When a new **foal** learns a person's smell and voice it will trust that person. Horses learn in steps. Keep the steps simple. When one step is learned start the next step.

Horses respond better to kindness than to punishment. Always reward good behavior with praise. A rough tone of voice is used to correct bad behavior. Training should be fun for the horse. When it is fun the horse does not become bored and makes fewer mistakes.

Palominos learn more easily when they are young.
Training should be fun for the horse.

GLOSSARY

ANCESTOR (AN-ses-tor) - An animal from which other animals are descended.

BIT - The metal piece of a bridle that goes in the horse's mouth.

BREED - To produce young; also, a group of animals that look alike and have the same ancestor.

BRIDLE - The part of a horse's harness that fits over the head, used to guide or control the animal.

DEWORMING (de-WURM-ing) - To take away worms.

DOMESTICATED (doe-MES-tik-ay-ted) - To train to live with and be useful to humans.

ENGLISH SADDLE - A flat-seated saddle used for racing, jumping and polo.

EQUIPMENT (e-QWIP-ment) - Saddles and bridles.

FOAL - A young horse under one year old.

HOOF - A horse's foot.

MARE - A female horse.

MARKINGS - The white color on the head and legs.

MUZZLE - Part of the face that extends forward and includes the nose, mouth and jaws.

NURSE - To give milk to a baby at the breast.

NUTRITION (new-TRISH-un) - Food; nourishment.

PASTURE - A field used for the grazing of cattle, sheep, or other animals.

PREGNANT - Carrying a baby inside the body.

PROTEIN (PRO-teen) - A compound that is needed for growth and development.

QUARTER HORSE - A compact muscular saddle horse that can run at high speed for short distances.

REINS - Narrow straps attached to a bit at either side of the horse's mouth and used to control the horse.

SADDLEBRED - A horse that is bred for riding.

THOROUGHBRED (THIR-oh-bred) - A horse descended from a breed first developed at the end of the eighteenth century by crossing English mares with Arabian stallions. They are trained for horse racing.

TRAINING - To teach.

WEANLING - What a foal is called after it is weaned.

WESTERN SADDLE - A strong saddle used by cowboys.

BIBLIOGRAPHY

Millar, Jane. *Birth of a Foal.* J.B. Lippincott Company, New York, 1977.

Patent, Dorothy Hinshaw. *A Horse of a Different Color.* Dodd, Mead and Company, New York, 1988.
———.*Horses of America.* Holiday House, New York, 1981.

Possell, Elsa. *Horses.* Childrens Press, Chicago, 1961.

Index

3918

PLEASSHARE YOUR THOUGHTS
ON THIS BOOK:

COMMENTS: Ican't say How much I ve horses and this book!	COMMENTS: I Love horses and this book!
COMMENTS: It was great	COMMENTS:
COMMENTS: I gave me info ot my repor	COMMENTS:
COMMENTS: nice inforan!	COMMENTS:
COMMENTS: Execlent and told m info	COMMENTS:
MMENTS: nk the boo great!	COMMENTS: